# The Still Position

*a verse memoir of my mother's death*

## Other works by Barbara Blatner

*No Star Shines Sharper,* a verse play (Baker's Plays)
*The Pope in Space,* poems (Intertext Press)
*Living with You* (NYQ Books, forthcoming 2010)

# The Still Position

*a verse memoir of my mother's death*

Barbara Blatner

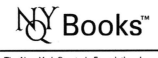

The New York Quarterly Foundation, Inc.
New York, New York

NYQ Books™ is an imprint of The New York Quarterly Foundation, Inc.

The New York Quarterly Foundation, Inc.
P. O. Box 2015
Old Chelsea Station
New York, NY 10113

www.nyqbooks.org

Acknowledgement:
"fact is" and "cruelties of the sun" were previously published in *Beloved on this Earth, an Anthology of Grief and Gratitude*, Holy Cow! Press, 2009.

First Edition

Set in New Baskerville

Layout and Design by Raymond P. Hammond

Cover art: "Snowy Field," 36 x 46 inches, charcoal on paper
© 1999 Katherine Meyer

Author photo © 2010 Lesley Eringer | www.neoimages.com

Library of Congress Control Number: 2010927577

ISBN: 978-1-935520-23-8

# The Still Position

*a verse memoir of my mother's death*

# Acknowledgements

I thank all those who have contributed to this book's birth: Denny Bergman for critiquing the manuscript; Andrew Grobman, Gerrit Lansing, Susan Donnelly, Suzanne Quall, Bruce Colbert, Sabra Loomis, Elizabeth Greywolf, Katherine Burger, Rosanna Yamagiwa Alfaro, Carole Rosenthal for reading or hearing the poems with appreciation; Amanda J. Bradley for her poems, her assistance, and for leading me to NYQ Books; NYQ Books Editor Raymond Hammond for his poet's heart and civil irreverence; the Virginia Center for the Arts and the Byrdcliffe Arts Colony for providing me time to work these poems; Bill Rainbolt for his generous suggestions; Katherine Meyer for her stunning cover drawing; Larry Lane for ongoing alive conversation, for savagery, for holding the bar consistently high; Monique Pommier for wise counsel and playful companionship on a parallel path; Lesley Eringer for many years of artistic comradeship, invaluable friendship and love.

I thank my mother for being so unapologetically who she was, and Sadie and Crow for nursing her to the end; my sister Mary Valentis for her daily care of and friendship with our mother, and for the creative intensity of her life and work; my brother Tom Blatner whose steadfast support of our mother shows his unique heart and wide mind; both Mary and Tom for their commitment to our bond and for living through our mother's death in March 1995; John Valentis and Jean Holtz for their presence during those days.

Finally, I thank my husband Arthur Dutton who meditated with a tender heart at my mother's bedside, fed her morphine in her last hours with exquisite gentleness, and without whose love, literary intelligence and support this book would not be in your hands.

*These poems, which tell the story of my mother's last five days, are dedicated to my family.*

# Contents

## Wednesday

## Thursday

## Friday

## 3. after

The characters in these poems are very real people and animals:

Betty—my mother
Arthur—my husband
Mary—my sister
Tom—my brother
Jean—Tom's partner at the time
Sadie—Betty's live-in caretaker
Crow—Sadie's husband
Amanda—Betty's white Samoyed dog
Max and Minnie—Betty's black cats

# 1. before

# home!

finally
home!
from the hospital
where old age
sickness
and death
stink
from anonymity.
home!
from your double-glassed
third floor
window full
of too much
sky, loud
sun and a
distant row
of skinny
parking lot trees.
home! and
by your own words
never
to return
to those
sharp white
corridors again,
though
it means
what we all know
it means—
a quicker
dying.

but home!
finally

to know yourself
at the bone
nearly
bare of time,
doomed and
protected
in your own
bed under
blue and
white quilted
covers,
and as you
lie in that
familiar
place,
to gaze
out the sliding
glass door
onto wide
whitish lawn
of early spring
where sky
throws its
palest light
and your two-hundred-year old
apple tree,
bitten almost
in half
last year
by lightning,
stands, branches bare
now, scored
twisted

and barren,
and finally
to imagine
fresh taffeta
frothing
from its moist boles
in a May
you will not
see, infant
blossoms
on ancient
limbs

## living room

less than three weeks till you come to death but what a
beginning:

Tom stations you in living room chair at western windows,
glass walls pointing a wide prow over snow-bare back lawn
toward stony crest of mountain scrolled above woods and
orchards.   early March afternoon not spring not winter,
chilly but a baby sun buds on the rim of the mountain,
warms your tented shoulders, steepening cheekbones,
yellowing weed of hair as you nod at a few last visitors and
gaze for what will be the last time at that blue-ringed moun-
tain.  you've moved closer to death it's clear, you turn to
us from the mountain, you're beautiful surrendered, the old
hardness the *no* to love the schoolgirl shyness has broken
inside you, a mild trusting radiance lights your eyes your
bones

and when I go to hug you, you reach for me you let me have
you you're a smiling child

## grotesque

at your house last summer
I'm reading, futon on
floor.  you wander in
begin scratching yes
scratching! one crooked
finger like an obsessive
hen, the nude mattress
   on the adjacent bed.

"mild alcohol-related dementia,"
said the doctors
after you landed in the
hospital smudged by a small
stroke and they pried you
from your liquor—60 yrs,
two daily glasses of gin—
enough to drown forever
several volumes of brain.

first you forgot
how to play bridge, write
checks, then pieces of alphabet,
then you sideswiped
a few parking lot
cars and lost your way
driving home
before Mary Tom
and I, your three kids in age-
descending order, pocketed
your keys, "for your own good,"
and hired live-in keepers,
Sadie and Crow.

you who seduced us
with brilliantly neurotic
charm, snowed us time
after time on
the golf course winning with the swing
of an angel, wowed us
with your passionate lazy
liberal politics and chess games
that bore on for years via
long-distance mail
with your brother,

you who knew how to draw
our empathy like blood
for your faithless marriage, poverty
of confidence, touchy
shyness, seamy love affairs,
lost wealth, childishness with
money, you the perfectly unwilling
perfectly longed-for mother

is now scratching, scratching!

I feign deadly calm:
"What are you doing?"
"Getting the bed ready for you,"
you say, scratching.

how purely rusted how gone
you are from me now
who never really had you, and

I want to kill you, mom,
in my mind, that is, and
the mind is sure a killer.

I take a deep breath.

ok.  I can
execute–toss you from my
heart like a useless
thing—or make room for
you, idiot daughter, mother
of my dreams.  I take a deep
wide breath

# Sadie and Crow

Mary, Tom and
I grew up
with cooks
gardeners
nurses, and
though the family
later lost its
money, you still
had enough
when you got
sick for us to
hire from
an eighth-inch
ad in the
village paper
Sadie and Crow,
a sixtyish
vagabond couple
from the working
welfare
poor,
to live with you,
care for you.

and we think
we got a
deal, we
once-wealthy
over-schooled
middle-aging
uptight
emotional
"professionals,"

because Sadie,
five-foot
aging owlet, vague
glasses, peppery
cap of hair,
talking
laughing crying
voice always
scratching
for the root
of an ancient
sorrow,
is tireless
—though exhausted—
from the beginning,
cooking cleaning
scheduling shopping
fretting for you,
later, dressing
you, and later,
bathing you, and
lately sitting up
through the night
with you.

while Crawford,
tall doughy
diabetic
polar bear
but gentle
so the claws
don't show,
who rides his gold

barka-lounger
for hours in
front of the
tube, folding
and unfolding
newspapers,
who never
edits the slow
melody of
failure
from his voice,
when you were
able, failed
faithful
knight that he is, drove
you and
your dogs to
doctor
hairdresser
store.

they probably
think they got
a deal too—
a place to live
a fortress
mountain
looming in back, happy
dogs to adopt
and a woman
who's dying
slowly but surely
dragging no

tubes bags or
needles, just
needing to be
kept clean, kept
smiling when
possible, and dosed
with food
and pills.

we—Mary, Tom
and I—and they—
Sadie and Crow—
kinda like each other
and kinda don't.
we all avoid
the little cliffs
the tensions—
how to cook, what
to buy, when
to spend–everything's
all right, as long as we
keep straight
who's getting
the best of whom.

well, who?
aren't we
in this death
together?

# Mom agonistes

close to noon
on Sunday
Arthur and I leave you
sitting in bed
biting at a spoon
of jello, Mary
and Sadie
fussing about.
an hour later,
as we cross
Berkshire hills
home to Boston,
it all comes
down,
as if everything
you've ever eaten
turns liquid,
and overwelling,
gushes through
your body
which like a broken
hydrant
lets go
streams of shit
over the bedclothes.

gently
Mary and Sadie
collapse you
onto the floor of
the shower.
too weak
to rise in

the torrent, pelted
by water,
you sit on
the tiles
the mud
flooding
out of you—
(later you tell Mary
you thought
you'd die there)—
but after they
pull you out, gripping the
rim of the sink
you claw your
way to stand
and cling there,
quaking with
will, on
heron legs,
and still the hot
muck pours
out of you.

meanwhile
nature and machine
flow on.  outside
your bathroom
window, cats
Max and Minnie
jump bugs
on the cold grass,
and red
sumac cones

chandelier their tree.
out front
cars whizz
the country road
and two miles
down the MOBIL
station sells fuel
and videos.
at a Turnpike
Roy Rogers we
eat hamburgers
and coke, as earth
tears through your
body, as Sunday
empties you
forever

# sunday

suddenly world's too huge, a vaulted silence, after a three-hour drive from your house home to Boston thinking you're pretty all right, Mary's message on the machine turns us round now we're back tracing asphalt on the Pike Natick Worcester Springfield ashen Berkshire miles

at dusk we cross into NY crest hill above your native Albany, faraway ghost rise of last hospital you lay in, then junket off highway head out of town in shallow darkness, lawns and fields where gleams of snow ebb from drowned spring soil oh deafening tide of change

as night falls we're into your territory grocery store Mobil station derelict cow farm with poetic view of blue-black mountains, March land old snow new dust orchard then swamp doused in older-than-human silence finally we turn down the long curve of gravel drive.

Sadie at the yellow-lit kitchen door, then down the dark hall we step over Amanda your beloved white dog and into your room:

tremulous lamplight.

hollow-cheeked you lie, eyes toward us.

world contracts to a single bed

29

2.

# Monday

# as you lay dying


*damn pity*
say your eyes.
these days
you'll suck savor
from what's
left.
so for hours
this afternoon
you watch videos
of Pavarotti
your darling
thrush
bursting in tux
in concert hall
Milan Beijing Paris
an orchestra moving
behind him
    *what the hell*
says your girl
of a smile,
you whose flesh
is so subtracted
limbs and
hips so
narrowed
bone could easily
breach
skin,
still you raise
one dried
branch of
arm to
conduct
from your fallow
bed the whole

shebang,
commanding
every part
of your
fat bird
Pavarotti's
heart
to open
and fly
into song,
and by your brave
withered
baton, he
whose voice
makes love
the bravest
thing, weeping
a hankie
to his lips
and brow,
pours out to
you alone
full-throttled
songs.
death's
horizon is
puny, life's
sky wider
than ever.
    "turn it up"
you rasp
    "give me Pavarotti
    or nothing"

# fact is

I stare
out your kitchen window
at green-black
mountain swelling
above back yard
fields and orchards.

near the summit's
stony escarpment
before the vertical scar
cut through trees
for telephone wire,
a hawk
is flying.

and I'm thinking:
it doesn't matter
that you neglected us
got drunk at us
charmed us
divided us
against each other.
we love you terribly,
the eye of love's
ever sharper
now that you lie
in bed in your room
at the end of the hall
dying.

we're bound to you
like that hawk
to her hunger,

we hunt
your love
we circle
we shadow

# table

by the wall near your bed
stands a table with
hourglass-shaped surface,
once ruffle-skirted
vanity table where I primped
at thirteen, opening
drawers to a private
chaos of eyeshadows
lavender teal sky-blue,
swarms of hair pins
pony tail fasteners,
stashes of powders,
colonies of tiny
lipsticks

      how many hours
I sat in my gauzy bathrobe
before the triptych
mirror, vaguely dreaming
at some great
threshold, gazing
at my face,
at my breasts
cupping them in my
hands, pushing them
high.  oh the ripeness
and thickets of terror
I'd encounter
invoking the rhythm
of hands moving
over flesh.

now the table, stripped
of bride-white paint,
shorn of ruffle and mirror,
serves your death
it's a hospital tray
arranged with amber
pill bottles, plastic
cups, shining scissors,
boxes of swabs, fat
geriatric diapers—
everything public
fatally clean
evoking your body's
chaos.

and as you lie
in bed, flat and
hairless, little more
than skin-wrapped bone,
face carved by
hollows, lips palest
pottery brown, almost
cured of moisture,
your eyes seek
no mirror but move
with sure economy
to what they know,
o the ripeness
the thickets of terror
you must encounter
at some great threshold
vaguely dreaming

# expanding universe

boy were you
enraged when
Sadie and Crow
moved into the
house where you'd
lived alone
twenty years.
it was class
conflict in a clash
of tastes, e.g.,
moneyed
once, you insisted
on sirloin
rare while Sadie
turned up her nose,
"it's too fancy,"
she sniffed
and killed your filet
for an hour
in Heinz.
    yes it was Sadie
who maddened you
with endless
scratchy discourses,
Sadie who despoiled
your bathrooms
with knitted
chatskis of
bears and elephants,
it's Sadie
who sails in
with Crow
from shopping odysseys

four hours after she
promised, every time.
     but it was
Sadie who mopped
shit from the floor
the day it spilled from your crater
like lava, Sadie
who doesn't pretend
like everyone else
you don't wear
diapers, Sadie
who sits up
nights with you,
nodding at your
secrets, guarding
your bed with her
shadow, and
it's only Sadie
you let wash you now, head
to toe, and velcro
a new diaper on.
     yes it's Sadie
you've completely
come round to,
Sadie messy
in matters of heart,
unschooled in self-
suppression, who stops
Mary Tom me
in kitchen or hallway
with a hand on the arm,
and with a teary

"I love her
I love your mother,"
turns us
to love's abyss

# invisible bodies

*God will need something to burn...*
—Jane Kenyon

five days
before your last,
near where you lie
too proud
or terrified
to say "I'm dying,"
and dying anyway,

I jog solo
in flocked shadows
of mountain
over pale March field
flashing a few
crows and turreted by a
flat mounded hill
where Mohawks
once buried their dead,

come across
greenish-white
deer bones—lank
tibia, chunky
vertebrae, sickle
ribs–scattered
on the matted grass.

flesh and blood
was their story,
then a blaze
of death, plot unknown,
seared away all

detail save these
chalky runes:
something
to read
into.

I kneel
and stare:

*let them*
*signify*

a world of mercy
for my tears,
a clean leap
of fire
for you

# Tuesday

## your vision

6:30 am, just gave you serum
to cotton your brain
a while to stop bleeping
little zealots of pain
to your nerve endings.

I'm sitting on the bed
I face you, hold your hand
watch you
doze into the clouds,
Sadie's in a chair alongside.

I gaze hard at
your colorless lips,
heavy-lidded eyes
when a thought
shoots straight across
my forehead, taut
and bright I swear
like a silver wire:

*give her what she needs.*

a moment later
really a moment
you open shining eyes.

"a vision," you smile.
"Barbara give me a vision."

"what?!" we ask in
amazement. "what did
you see?"

then you tried but
could only mutter
"vision," before the drug
fastened you to sleep.

why should you try to
say what you saw?
there's hardly
world left or time
for you to answer
what the living insist on.
the rough smooth stones,
words you carried,
are almost gone

# dehydration

all you'll touch is gingerale
or that sugary raspberry
goop pointed down the pink
hole of your mouth
through a plastic straw
with bendable girdle
or dribbled down
your raw vermillion throat
with a spoon.

for weeks you've taken
so little from the world—
three bites of meat,
a quarter baked potato,
less than a baby bird
would eat,
and for the past week,
no solids, just liquid
ration–Canada Dry, Juicy Juice.

now it's down to
the raspberry stuff
sip by sip.   your body
emptying itself of moisture
reminds me how much we are
made of water.  now your ocean's
winching back, drop
by drop, bucket
by bucket, into
the old kettle sun.

sweet christ, today
your lips drag
back from your teeth
and the horny
skull begins to beach

## revenge fantasy

late afternoon
I pause near your bed
no one's around.

you sigh in your sleep,
your small skiff body
swamped by covers.
one weathered arm's
flung above your head
like a sprained
oar.  in a few days,
you'll stop moving.

I stare at your
sunken face, listen
for the weak
lapping of breath,
caught in a thought:

I could simply
kill you now,
get it over with,
who would
know the difference?
I could easily
kick you in, stove you
under, for all those times,
mean on gin,
you rammed words
into my belly.

the thing is:
I can't hate you

more than a
minute.  after
all the betrayals,
my affection never
idles, not even
down to indifference
and there's nothing
I can do about it.

love's the drowning
watch I keep
I watch you sleep

# drink

in your pity-proof
Kate Hepburn face
girlish even in its
last frame,

in your flesh
drawn so tight
since bowel surgery
two months before
your pubic hair
didn't grow back in,

in your sheared
bladed-with-bone
diaperpad-beneath-you body
into which
in nine days time
you haven't
put a solid thing—

take the glass please
with twiggy
   fingers,
use two hands,
lift head off pillow,
lips to rim—

now drink! drink!
it's that red goop
you're crazy
about, it's
sugar water
water everywhere,

and if you take
just one sip
we'll be happy.
then, mom,
if you'll proceed to
swallow—we know it's hard—
if you'll make
that decision deep
in your throat—
we'll be very
happy

## some last phrases

with four days
to live in, pleasures
are few.  those
you've kept
you whet
on the sharpest
stone.  one's
that ruby-red liquid                "so delicious!"
you love so much,
only thing that's gone
down for days beside pills.

another's
the big fluffy white
dog of your heart Amanda.        "isn't she terribly wonderful?"

one more's
Pavarotti,
portly thrush
who trills to you
for hours
from VCR/TV.                "I adore  Pavarotti!"

the channels of bliss
deepen

# body language

always,
and always
so quick
to admit it,
you were too
uptight too
emotionally
arthritic
to hug me,
too weak
for the strenuous
sweetness
of "I love you,"
too delicate
for the fat
of a
compliment,
taken or given.
you loved us yes
but needed us
more—that
was the real
infirmity.

even as an adult
I'd query:
"do you love me?"
and always
"you know I do
do I have to say it?"
was your reply.
so what's
happening now

four days
before you
die?  I sit
on your bed
you clasp
my hand
deliberate
as a priest,
say "hi babe!"
with a smile
shot
into my eyes—
a dose
of radiance
that breaks
into me,
for a moment
you're really
mother,
you mean to
give me
breath, to
lift me.
is death
making you
hearty?

# Wednesday

# wednesday

your smile
after you drink
pierces
like the high
d of Bach's
orchestral horn.

Arthur and I
stand by your bed
gawking.
face it:
we love you.

you gaze back
square
a moment
then, under your breath,
matter of fact:
"you're lucky."

and that's it
that's all
the expression
all these sorrowful weeks
of any tune of
regret that might play
around your heart.

lucky?

well,
30 years younger
than you, a "lovely"

couple, and some days
alive, meaning
we carry on
with the music,
and that's plenty.

but if time is
music, music
is marrow:
what we hear of you
dies away
day after tomorrow

# time shadows

standing round your bed
me Arthur Mary Sadie Jean Tom
like crows at a patch of flesh
our eyes feed on what's left:

face still beautiful but too tightly
sculpted, hands and arms
singed with lavender bruises,
under the white flannel gown, stick bones
tent a skin hovel.

still, as you return our gaze
around the circle
your brown eyes are steady.

if we could only hold you
here right here fix
this moment forever
we wouldn't want for food.

but you're no fool, you
see our hunger.
"don't look at me like that,"
you say, "you make me
think I'm dying"

## "childhood is the kingdom where nobody dies"
*—Edna St. Vincent Millay*


this final scene
of your life
you play
against humiliation
as if dying's
a clown's craft
a pratfall
a staged loss of
footing, merely
a scene
of surrender.

when we were
kids, you wouldn't
take us to
funerals.
"other people die, but we're not gonna," Tom
and I chanted
at eleven and
nine, then
died
into puberty.

who are you kidding?

for 6 months
you've worn
diapers. Sunday
you couldn't
stop shitting.
today we hoist
your head
from the pillow,

squeeze
a few beads
of water
down your throat.

still your show
goes on.

for god's sake,
can you give us
a sign
that you know
dying
is what
you're doing?
for once in
your life
take life on

# deer!

each day you
sleep in bed a
denser sleep
not two days left
to live in.
I stare out
your kitchen window,
hands in dishwater,
at your late March
front lawn's
broad arc
of ghostly grass.
suddenly–
what's that?
on a balding patch
near the gravelled
drive—I'm going nuts!
but there they are—
gauzy wingtips
raised to
fly—a pair of—
four-foot high
beigy
butterflies?!

wait a minute
—look again—
another second and—
it's not butterflies–it's
—deer?  yes!
deer! three of them
nose the scrufty grass!
look again—standing

out before the
bushes in front of
the dark woodshed—
three more!
but look again—
further left
near your
bedroom window
by your lightning-
cleft apple tree—
two more—eight in all!
seven does, one
young antlered
buck grazing
the lawn—must be
the herd you
and Sadie
raved about
but always spotted
back of the house,
cautious at rim
of woods
in mountain's
shadow—never
have they
come, bold apparitions,
anywhere near
the front lawn…

but they're here
they're here!
noses to grass, moving
if at all

by shrug of tail
or rephrasing
a charcoal hoof.

I call
through the house
"Look out, stand still!"
for if we move
too quickly
in this place
of windows,
one or two lift
slow eyes
to question and stare.

please let them
stay so you
can see them.
you'll have to
wake up now
you'll have to
want to, you'll
have to lift
your head
too

# butterflies?!

did I really see
four-foot
mauvey butterflies
chiffoning the lawn,
wings pointed skyward
poised to sail?

must be
grief for you
smudges my sight
or I'm really
going crazy!

then again,
to the Greeks
butterflies did the work
of death.  sticking
to a corpse
on the highway
for the sweet
sluice of blood, they'd rise
and scatter in a
cloud, the flocked
soul lifting from one
shroud, the Greeks said

# the buck on the lawn

Friday
you'll come to
it—last breath.
but late Wednesday afternoon
you lace
hands
behind neck,
raise your head
to watch
a young buck
with new forest
on his brow
pause
under your bare
ancient apple tree.

you're careful
and proud
as he is.
but after all,
your death's
just
a fact,
not poetry
like this antlered
prince
lifting his
head like he
owned
the world
and all time
in it.

Millay's
"Buck in the Snow"
was just about
your favorite
poem
and one of
the only
times your voice
bolted out
straight and clear,
as you read
to us again
and again
how the legs
of the gunshot animal
buckled
under the heavy
hemlocks,
"…his wild blood scalding the snow…"
while already far away
"How strange a thing …" life looked out
"…attentive from the eyes of the doe…"
so even as kids
we knew
you were
in love with
that animal
and its death.

today
the maple eyes
of the buck
who ambles

right up to your
sliding-glass door
are
attentive.
your smile
I imagine
is saying:
*ok, I'm going.*
*but look*
*what's come,*
*look what's come*
"with long leaps lovely and slow,"

just as
you are falling—"How strange a thing is death"—
in slow
motion
in your own
wilderness

# clown

just when I think
you're too childish
for truth, with a
rattle for a mind,

I hear how last week
with elegant '50's
Jewish bravado
you quizzed
the visiting nurse:
"is there anything
you can do
with this mess?"
("mess" meaning
your body)
and got your
answer
and let it fly
wild around
inside you
without a sound.

in the meantime,
I keep waiting
for the emerald
conversation,
your deathbed
profession:
*I'm going*
*I love you*
*so long.*

instead you offer
no fanfare no
processional, just
the keen note
of a little smile.
comedy, the mask
of ignorance, is how
you'll meet the gods

## dying as trickery

"The dirty rat,"
Tom says.  "She's really
gonna do it."

## elemental

sick little
fish, flat
bruised,
time-
speckled,
slipping too
quickly
away from
us out of
the tide
onto fiery
sand,
you couldn't
give yourself
as mother,
only as friend
or daughter,
even then
you were
always
flashing
out of reach
with self-
deprecating
style.
    but these last
scorching
days of your life,
your body
a drought,
not shitting
pissing
eating
only drinking
drop
by drop,

you toss me
pure
oxygen
in a smile,
fasten Tom's
hand in
your own
a few times,
dub Mary
"general,"
finally
sounding
your approval
after nearly
50 years.
    old minnow,
death
the great
relaxer
softens
your belly.
from the
furnace
sand and
brilliant air
that drowns you,
with heart's
last gasp,
will's last
muscle,
you flash
love
signals

## beginning the end

late Wednesday night
just as the nurse predicted,
from malnutrition
dehydration
kidney poisons,
pain catches up to you
its locomotive
shrieking
down the tracks.
Tom Jean and
Sadie are there
when you start
yelling, trying to
run from your
body.  they grab
the amber
vial of morphine
the nurse left
for this very hour,
and feed it down
your throat
to cotton you
against the oncoming
shrill.  all night
they administer the
priceless oil.
your cries were
terrible, Tom reported,
but near morning
grew fainter
as gradually the
jewel-colored poison
sent its news

dazed your throat
reshuffled your breathing.
by Thursday morning,
when Arthur and I
take over, you lie
on your side, deep-
sleeping, lungs
working a numb
steady breathing,
pain's whistle dim
in the distance.
but surely
now death steadies on
with a noiseless roar

# Thursday

# wizards of relief

every two hours
we gather
your broken
birdbody
in our arms.

each time
you're more gone,
each time
Arthur calls
more tenderly,
deliberately:
"Betty, Betty, we're going to give you
something for the pain,"

till you whimper
and crack
your lips,
sneer them back
from horsey teeth—
that's all
the effort left
in your body—
and he drops it
down, the honey-
colored morphine
with a four-inch
dropper capped
with black
rubber
lays it in
your throat.
at this final

grazing
ground, this
nest, you can't
swallow anymore,
but when it
runs down
the hatch
the swallowing
reflex
takes over.

through the day and night,
against roar
of cell on
cell, blade
on blade,
we hold you, baby bird,
we feed you
against pain's
will, of your
own will
we absolve you,
and there's
nothing
tragic
about it

# human log

with each
2-hour dose
of morphine
you need to be shifted
in bed from one
side to the other
because bone
can easily slip
through skin—
it's pastry-delicate.

here's the routine:
one of us stands
on either
side, we lift
the towel
under the sheet
that's under you,
jostle it
into a hammock,
like a firewood
carrier, then
as you fire us
with screams, with
conflagration,
carefully carefully
we turn you,
our burning
cargo.

the first 16 hours
on morphine
when we turned you
you screamed.
after that, the drug
found you,
doused
the flame,
took you in

# last words from the queen

way out on morphine
almost 18 hours,
four in the afternoon
you're on your back
eyes clapped shut
voice down a hole
somewhere.

in the next room
Tom and Sadie squabble
something
petty about you.

suddenly, a
voice—whose voice?
"You two get in here!"

astounded, they go
to your room.

jesus! your eyes are open
fire runs in them
sharp as light
on a mountain stream.

"What are you two fighting about?"

their mouths hang open.

again:
"What are you fighting about?!"

"Something about work,"
Tom lies quickly.

"Do you think I'm stupid?!"
this almost a roar.

silence.

then you say
to your son:
"Don't be an ass,"
and close your eyes
close yourself down
once more.

these last words—
like a legend on a banner
were handed to Tom,
but belong to all of us
petty squabblers
who know how
mean spoiled arbitrary
you can be
and how
dead on

# fight!

we grew up rich
fighting over roast beef bones
like there wasn't enough
to go around.
later we lost our money
but we're still fighting
over bones, a graduated
pile, you, mom,
it was always you,
and as you lie in a morphine
stupor, one day to
go, the old grief's near rabid,
losing what it gnawed upon.
of course I don't
know how it started.
suddenly Mary's shrieking
she's pushing me
by my shoulders
I'm pushing back
she's out the door
into the car roaring up
dust down the driveway.
then Tom won't talk to me
for hours.  so that last
night of your life,
horrifying Arthur, I take the car
and drive like heavy
lightning in darkness
down country roads
thinking it might be nice
to explode the car
on a fat pine tree
ancient and grooved.

next morning
moments after
your final breath
it's like that violence
never happened, the three of us
huddle on the porch
in mourning, arms
circle each other, still bound
to seek and later seek love's
flesh and bone.  in
the meantime, you're gone

# morphine

the first 16 hours
on the drug
you yelp and curse
when we turn you,
don't actually yell
"don't touch me!" or
"damn you!"
but your screams
raise reproach
like a spear,
pierce me
with an old
guilt, irrational,
the worst kind—
that I must be
damned
for hurting you.
    but that's
history,
gotta be.
here, now,
you're most pitiful
and I must
understand
that your cries
hurl from
wounds
of your own
and fall short
of me.  whatever
you are
and have been
is to forgive,

so with the sweet
milk sorrow
of forgiveness,
with Arthur and Sadie
I minister
to you,
lead you
through pain
out of pain
where you need
to be,
until
as post-
midnight
hours accrue, I
can't do it
anymore
and stand back
from the
bed, stupid
with awe
and sorrow
as more
and more
I see
your torment
is a place
you alone
climb
through.
    so really
that long
final night,

as your screams
subside,
it is you
who shepherd us
up an invisible
stony path,
your spear
of pain blunted
to a staff
of grief.  we are
your death's
sheep

# Friday

# from a book of hours

6 am
Friday morning
stillness wakes me.

I sit up in bed,
struck
by what I can't
hear,

stare out window
as if at an illuminated manuscript

I could look at forever
just this page:

blue-gold sky, fresh cloud,
emerald-black mountain, trees
on rocky ledges,

on the summit, the tiny pin
of telephone tower—all

brilliantly clear,
in shadow and out,

and on the lawn below, at page
bottom, a few melting
blazons of spring snow

and on and through
everything
everywhere
the sun shines
without reservation.

then words
in the hallway—
something…something… "coma."

I go to your room.

you're alone,
on your left side,
eyes latched, cheek to pillow,

still breathing,
an ashy breathing, like
a shuttle of leaves.

so finely
drawn into
the hour of this book

you're locked
in a paradise
I can't remember

## last breath

sunny Friday
9:45 am

I try to sleep
but Arthur calls.

where you curl
on your left side
we stand by:

one breath, like
dewlap of iris, fragrant
with ephemeral.

then a lapse
an infinity–time
is that close.

then another breath,
thinnest veil, patient,
no longing.

and a second rest,
cocooned
tighter
than the first.

then a third breath
lightly scrolled
doesn't quite
unfurl.

and a third
pause.

and pause

endures

# the still position

the left cheek cools
on the pillow.
the right we
almost see hollowing,
the cast of the
face, still classic,
grows harder,
going yellow.

the shut eyes—
I touch them—
two humped shells,
pearly brink
of cornea
under one lid.

where the open
eyes would be
pointing:
Mary's bridal
photo props
on the bedside
table—snowy
veil, eyes lips hair
darkly radiant.

toward that beloved
face the tiny
body curls,
bones sculpting
the blue and
white cover.

Tom and I sit
near the foot of
the bed, keeping
watch. we swear
we almost see
that quilt rising
and falling.

it isn't

# verification

about an hour
after you stop
breathing, a nurse
with blond hair
and hippie pants
comes quietly
in a beige sedan.

Sadie and I
stand across the room
from the bed
as if
at a great
distance, watch
her touch
your yellowy forehead
with her palm,

raise the cover,
lift your talon
of a hand,
its small points
curving downward,
nip wrist
between thumb
and forefinger
and wait for a beat—

then lean and press
the stethoscope's
thick coin
to your chest,
never moving you

from the still position,
and listen
for the remote
ranking
of a heart
in its chamber.

does she hear something...?
maybe she hears something...

"I don't find
any pulse
or heartbeat,"
she says
and straightens
and covers you again.

oh.
she heard it,
too—no waters
coursing, canyon
empty, sun
soundless—
and the beast
your life
nowhere
hiding

# 3. after

# theatre of death

if mortality smells,
there's no
whiff of it here.

they clean got you,
the officials
we scripted in
a week ago:

the nurse who
softly verified
death,

the dead-eyed
men who carried
your prize
bones in a red velvet
sack over
frozen lawn
to hearse,

the same
who in slate suits
gangstered
your coffin
from hearse
to surgical grave,

finally,
the rabbi

107

we'd just met
intoning his
Sunday morning
burial schtick.

why did we let you go,
who had you
so much
in our arms
these past days?

why didn't we take you
to the woods
back of your house,
to the clearing
that looks over
slate stone wall
to an ocean of
field and green-black
torrent of
mountain?

why didn't we
take you
where deer walk
and hawks rise
to the escarpment
and dig a hole
in cool
March ground?

we could have
covered you
we could have
held you
till the planet
held you down

# causes of death (a backwards chronology)

congestive heart failure
obstructed breathing
mucus in lungs
kidney failure
toxified blood
60 years of anger at brother
dehydration
difficulty urinating
malnutrition
intestinal malfunction
rage
diarrhea
waning hope of living
stomach operation
hospitalizations
blocked intestines
minor strokes
stopping drinking
fear, humiliation
living alone
alcohol-induced dementia
liver damage
hospitalization
boyfriend's death (Mortie, 92 yrs old)
alcoholism (50-plus yrs: 2 or more gins a day)
social phobia
narcolepsy (25 yrs on benzedrine/dexedrine, 20 yrs on ritalin)
repressed love
right-wing politics (of others)
heart racing (tachycardia)
toe gout
mild arthritis
overinvolvement with three children
mild skin cancer (too much golf course sun)
anti-Semitism

being Jewish
stomach ulcer operation
hospitalization
stomach ulcer
death of pets
fear of success, fear of writing
living alone
loss of family wealth
divorce
intestinal blockage and operation
hospitalization
long tumultuous extramarital affair
living with others
lack of voice in family business
marital separation
domestic violence
overattachment to children
repressed rage
two miscarriages
stillborn twins
faithless husband
lack of confidence
cigarettes (60 yrs)
early death of father
infantilized by nurse
early wealth
flamboyant, possessive mother
sexual molestation by older brother?
loved, feared by brothers
enlarged heart
rheumatic fever
birth

## under the trees at the Jewish cemetery

seven of us line up lace together, every waist circled by an
arm.  you're on my left Mary I guess we're friends again?
Uncle Ira's on my other side.  March sun bites through the
leaves I want to shield my eyes but my hands aren't free.
workmen tamp down dirt along your finished grave.  the
rabbi, a stranger, bobs too close intones his lines we don't
know Hebrew.

suddenly he's reciting in English the "time for every season
under heaven" thing suddenly I'm sobbing soundlessly
you too Mary we're shaking from shoulders down.  but my
hands aren't free can't pull a tissue from my pocket.   so
when you turn to me Mary with the onyx poetry of it all in
your eye

you see a lanky rope of snot swinging from my nose a few
feet down, you see a great flag of mucus swaying in the
breeze.  your eyes widen and we're off! soundless hysterical
giggling, heads bowed.  Tom thinks we're grieving to cre-
scendo, tightens his grip around Mary.   no one knows till
later what we're shaking down

but mom, in your chestnut coffin, smart navy skirt silk
blouse spike heels silver necklace, of course you're laughing
like crazy you're cracking up you got a whole lotta shakin'
goin' on

# cruelties of the sun

lying in bed
this morning
two hundred miles
from your
house and lawn,
looking out the window, I can't see
the source of light
its bulb is burred
in fields of
cloud, but the power
of that sun is on,
gotta be, first week
of April, lemony
April, month
of your birth day.

so the legion
daffodils must be
shining down the margins
of your lawn
and all over the grass
by the entrance
to your road,
two and three clumped
everywhere,
ready for the vase
and the bee.

the guy who built your house
30 yrs ago planted
over twelve varieties
of the canary
flower. who'd imagine

there were so many
kinds to mime
the trumpet
sun, call it forth, so many
to come back
so soon so bright
from soil's
packed coffins.

this gauzed sun
will have to
bruise me into
day, days without you,
world without
end.  but year
after year
your daffodils
will sound up
easy swift
flotillas,
come as you are
in and
out of light

# I see it in my mind

mountain black rocky green escarpment sky stretched above
forever empty clauses lonely freedoms.  lawn roaming back
to woods where deer move among trees, flag tails up and
down as if questioning something.  there's nothing to ques-
tion.  stars arrive at night over the house the picture win-
dows are thin membrane against dark.  the ache of it sings
to me inaudible bounded by the remains what lies around.
what do you do with absence

voices not pitched only at night more in sunlight not that
it's cruel but it's cruel reveals patterns of leaf and grass-
blade.  I sit in our yard 200 miles from your house sit in sun
under lilacs' burnt blossoms second day past summer sol-
stice light spills stronger breaks over its own prow day light
to crack the hour

I see you tending your garden bending at the waist solitary
paces to find there long sun camped on your shoulder
crows passing like charred skiffs above you the hawk's pas-
sage the hunting vortex winding higher and higher

## About the Author

Barbara Blatner is a poet, playwright and composer-musician. She lives in northern Manhattan with her husband and two cats, and teaches in the English Department at Yeshiva University. A second full-length collection of poems, *Living with You*, will be published by NYQ Books in Fall 2010. *The Pope in Space*, a poetry chapbook, was published by Intertext Press (1984). Barbara's verse play *No Star Shines Sharper* was published by Baker's Plays (1991), produced for radio and aired repeatedly on National Public Radio stations. Her plays have been produced in New York, Boston and Cleveland. She has written musical scores for theatre, including the Boston Shakespeare Company and New Theatre, and songs for the Boston-based fusion group Urban Myth with whom she played keyboards for five years.

# About NYQ Books™

NYQ Books™ was established in 2009 as an imprint of The New York Quarterly Foundation, Inc. Its mission is to augment the *New York Quarterly* poetry magazine by providing an additional venue for poets already published in the magazine. A lifelong dream of NYQ's founding editor, William Packard, NYQ Books™ has been made possible by both growing foundation support and new technology that was not available during William Packard's lifetime. We are proud to present these books to you and hope that you will continue to support The New York Quarterly Foundation, Inc. and our poets and that you will enjoy these other titles from NYQ Books™:

| | |
|---|---|
| Joanna Crispi | *Soldier in the Grass* |
| Ted Jonathan | *Bones and Jokes* |
| Amanda J. Bradley | *Hints and Allegations* |
| Grace Zabriskie | *Poems* |
| Ira Joe Fisher | *Songs from an Earlier Century* |
| Kevin Pilkington | *In the Eyes of a Dog* |

Please visit our website for these and other titles:

**www.nyqbooks.org**

Breinigsville, PA USA
30 January 2011
254380BV00001B/14/P